NATURE GOT THERE FIRST

NATURE GOT THERE FIRST

Phil Gates

KINGFISHER

NEW YORK

KINGFISHER
LONDON & NEW YORK

Copyright © Kingfisher 2010
Published in the United States by Kingfisher,
175 Fifth Ave., New York, NY 10010
Kingfisher is an imprint of
Macmillan Children's Books, London.
All rights reserved.

Distributed in the U.S. by Macmillan,
175 Fifth Ave., New York, NY 10010
Distributed in Canada by H.B. Fenn and Company Ltd.,
34 Nixon Road, Bolton, Ontario L7E 1W2

Library of Congress Cataloging-in-Publication data
has been applied for.

ISBN: 978-0-7534-6410-6

Kingfisher books are available for special promotions
and premiums. For details contact: Special Markets
Department, Macmillan, 175 Fifth Ave.,
New York, NY 10010.

For more information, please visit
www.kingfisherpublications.com

Printed in China
1 3 5 6 9 8 6 4 2
1TR/0310/TOPLF/140gsm/C

Contents

Inventions inspired by nature

▶ *Spacecraft flying above Earth's atmosphere are covered in white tiles to reflect the extreme heat from the sun. The skin of some desert lizards protects them in a similar way, by becoming lighter when the sun is at its hottest.*

Life is a natural experiment that began 3.5 billion years ago on Earth and is still in progress. During this period, evolution has produced a huge variety of adaptations in living organisms. Evolution is the gradual process by which all living things have changed since life first began. These adaptations have been tested in a kind of natural laboratory, or testing ground, that has exposed them to the most extreme physical conditions.

ADAPTING TO SURVIVE

The organisms that exist today do so because they are descendants of others that carried adaptations that allowed them to survive fires, ice ages, typhoons, drought, and even catastrophes such as those caused by asteroid impacts. No purely human inventions have ever been tested so thoroughly. It makes sense for us to copy the natural world's best features for our own use.

Velcro strip

◀▶ *The engineer George de Mestral realized how the hooked seedheads of plants such as burdock clung to the fur of passing animals, and he invented Velcro, a system of hooks and eyes that hold surfaces together but can easily be pulled apart.*

Velcro magnified

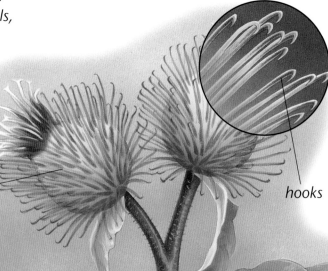

burdock

hooks

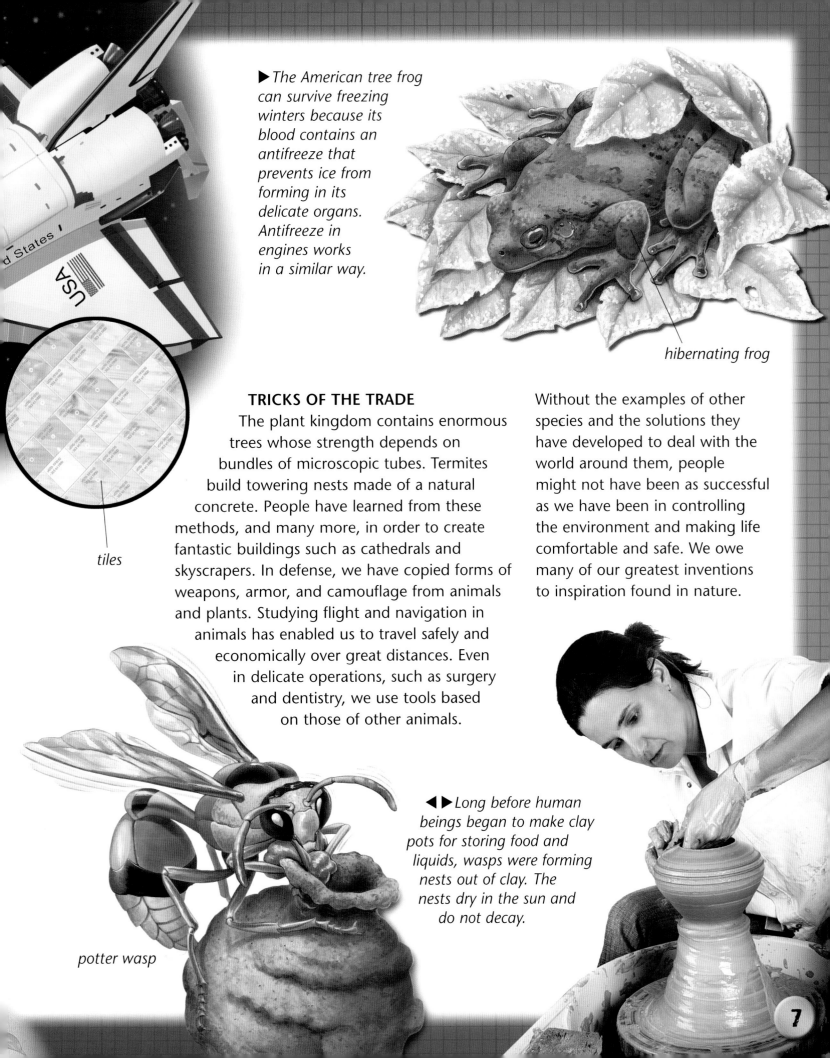

▶The American tree frog can survive freezing winters because its blood contains an antifreeze that prevents ice from forming in its delicate organs. Antifreeze in engines works in a similar way.

hibernating frog

tiles

TRICKS OF THE TRADE

The plant kingdom contains enormous trees whose strength depends on bundles of microscopic tubes. Termites build towering nests made of a natural concrete. People have learned from these methods, and many more, in order to create fantastic buildings such as cathedrals and skyscrapers. In defense, we have copied forms of weapons, armor, and camouflage from animals and plants. Studying flight and navigation in animals has enabled us to travel safely and economically over great distances. Even in delicate operations, such as surgery and dentistry, we use tools based on those of other animals.

Without the examples of other species and the solutions they have developed to deal with the world around them, people might not have been as successful as we have been in controlling the environment and making life comfortable and safe. We owe many of our greatest inventions to inspiration found in nature.

◀▶Long before human beings began to make clay pots for storing food and liquids, wasps were forming nests out of clay. The nests dry in the sun and do not decay.

potter wasp

Buildings

Large, complex structures need internal strengthening to counteract the forces that will act upon them when they are in use. Strength can come from the choice of materials, because some materials are stronger than others, or from the ways in which the materials are formed into parts and assembled. Cross bracing and other methods of load distribution are common in animals and plants.

BROAD AND TALL

Tropical rain forest trees may be over 165 ft. (50m) tall and have a heavy crown of branches and foliage. When high winds strike the top of a tree, enormous forces are transmitted to the base of the trunk and roots. But the tree is stabilized by great wooden buttresses, or supports, that broaden its base and stiffen its lower trunk.

buttresses

CATHEDRALS

Medieval architects used natural solutions to the problem of supporting the heavy stonework of their cathedrals. High walls, topped with heavy stone features, would bend under their own weight unless they were strengthened with thick buttresses, just like the stem buttresses of a tall tree.

Flying buttresses connect walls to solid towers at roof level.

I-beams

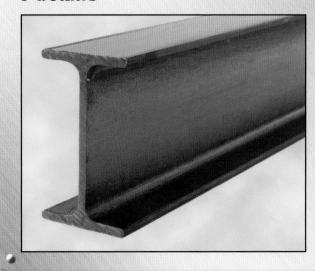

I-beams are a similar shape to the vertebrae in a dinosaur's spine. They are stronger and lighter than square beams. This shape was strong enough to support the weight of a dinosaur's body, and it works well for modern buildings, too.

This single vertebra from a dinosaur skeleton shows how similar its shape is to that of an I-beam.

RIBS AND SPACES

Birds have to be as light as possible in order to reduce the energy needed for flight. Many of their bones are filled with air spaces, but to keep rigid they have to have internal trusses and struts. This construction produces a good compromise between minimum weight and maximum strength.

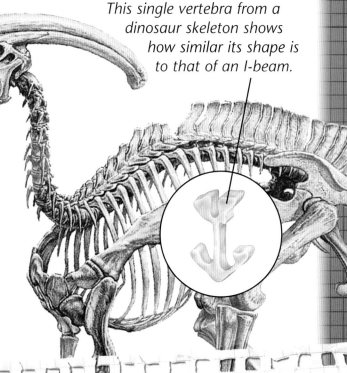

▲ Cathedrals are usually large, ornate structures. Strong, solid buttresses support the walls at ground level, and slimmer "flying" buttresses at the top help prevent the weight of the walls from pushing outward and keep them straight.

Airplane and bird wings

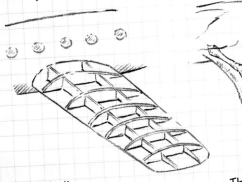

The hollow wings of an airplane are strengthened by spars.

The hollow bones in a bird's wing are strengthened by internal spars, too.

An airplane's weight must be kept to a minimum for flight, and its wings must be particularly strong. Wings are made from a series of ribs connected by spars and covered with a metal skin, producing a very light and strong structure.

Earth engineering

Animals that live in tunnels are hidden from many predators, but building underground requires special skills. Tunnels must be level and parallel to the surface. They must not flood or collapse, and they must have fresh air. For human builders, large dams and high-rise buildings became possible only when reinforced concrete construction methods were devised during the 20th century.

cutting head

DOGS THAT DIG

Prairie dogs are social animals that excavate huge networks of interconnecting tunnels. Good air circulation is essential, so they build volcano-shaped ventilation towers. These help draw currents of air through their underground cities.

BORING MACHINES

People build tunnels using enormous boring machines. The cutting head at the front slices through the rock and soil, and the waste material is mixed with water and pumped away. In order to draw air through the tunnel, an area of low pressure is created, and air under higher pressure moves toward the area of lower pressure. The Channel Tunnel between England and France runs for more than 31 mi. (50km) under the sea. Eleven boring machines were used in its construction.

ventilation shaft

propel cylinders
to move the
machine along

support legs

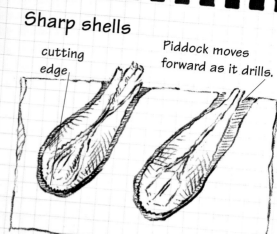

Sharp shells

cutting edge

Piddock moves forward as it drills.

Piddocks are bivalve mollusks, like mussels and razor clams. Their paired shells have fine teeth on their leading edge. Piddocks drill into solid rock by using their muscular foot to move their shell back and forth, wearing away a hole. A tunneling machine braces itself against the tunnel wall to create the force that pushes it into the rock. Piddocks brace themselves by growing in size as they dig.

SAFE AS HOUSES

Beavers dam small streams, creating a pond where they build a lodge of logs and turf to make an ideal home for their family groups. Their dams are so well engineered that they can last for centuries.

Water power

Humans build dams to create large lakes that contain millions of gallons of water. This large store of water is used in homes, factories, and farms. It can also provide a clean form of energy, which can be converted into electricity.

11

Natural materials

Only natural materials, such as stone, clay, and plant fibers, were available to early human cultures. Simple methods of weaving and pottery quickly became more complicated as civilizations developed. Animals build shelters to protect themselves from predators. Temporary nests are usually made from light, strong materials such as grass stems, which are easy to collect but decay (rot) quickly. Permanent homes are often made from wood or mud and are added to until they become massive structures that survive for years.

SKYSCRAPERS
In a skyscraper, built of steel, concrete, and glass, the entrance hall, dining rooms, and guest rooms are connected by elevators and stairs and are ventilated by ducts that circulate cool air through the building.

BUILDING WITH CEMENT
Termites build high-rise homes with a natural cement, using a mixture of saliva, sand, and excrement to make a material as hard as rock. Air shafts inside the termite mound draw air currents upward, keeping the millions of inhabitants cool. A large mound can rise to 23 ft. (7m) tall and can be demolished only with dynamite.

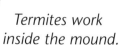

Termites work inside the mound.

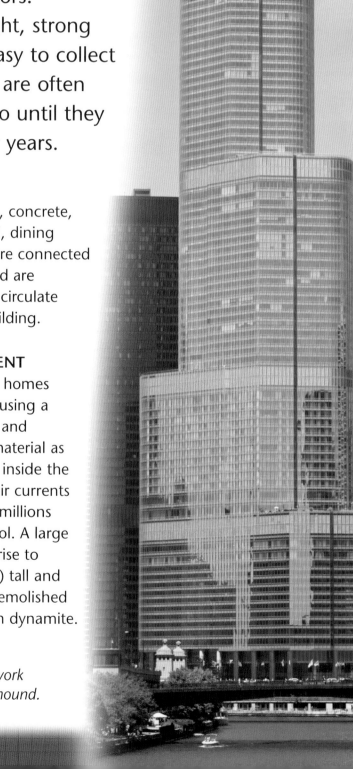

Weaving looms

People use weaving looms to weave cloth and rugs. They pass threads under and over each other on the loom using a piece of wood called a shuttle. This is exactly the same technique as the green tree ants use to weave their nests.

TREE ANTS

Green tree ants hold their young grubs (larvae) in their jaws and use the sticky, silken threads that the grubs produce to weave leaves together to make a nest. They are using their grubs like living shuttles.

POTTER WASPS

Potter wasps collect wet clay and mold it into a nest that can be used after it has dried in the heat of the sun. Nests made from mud do not decay and survive long after the young have hatched.

Potter wasps use their jaws to shape the wet clay.

POTTERY

Pottery is made from clay. Clay consists of wet soil particles that can be molded into shapes and then baked in a kiln. The earliest human potters probably built up wet clay into a pot, using much the same method as the potter wasp. Then, more than 700 years ago, potters in China developed technologies for baking clay at high temperatures to produce fine porcelain such as we use now.

Forming and shaping

Animals solve the problem of cutting, shaping, and drilling materials by using natural tools, such as flat, sharp-edged teeth and rough tongues, and twisting and turning motions that push pointed objects through soft materials. Our chisels, files, and drills provide very similar solutions to the same challenges. Such simple tools have led to many important advances in human civilization, from boat building to the construction of cities and machines.

SELF-PLANTERS

Oat seeds can plant themselves thanks to a natural drilling mechanism. A long bristlelike structure, called an awn, is attached to each seed. Awns are made of a material that coils and uncoils as it dries out, slowly drilling the seed into the soil.

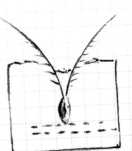

awn

fine hairs

CUTTING EDGE

Drills used for boring oil wells have teeth arranged around rotating wheels to cut through the rock. The friction that occurs between rock and teeth generates enormous heat, which is cooled by mud circulated down the center of the drill.

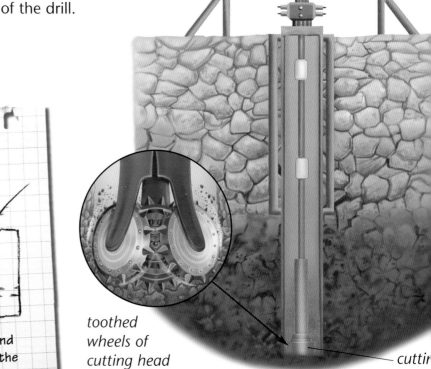

toothed wheels of cutting head

cuttir head

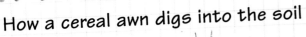

How a cereal awn digs into the soil

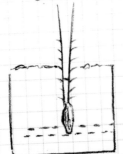

Dry awns bend during the day.

At night, dry awns straighten, driving the seed into the soil.

Awns dry and bend again the next day.

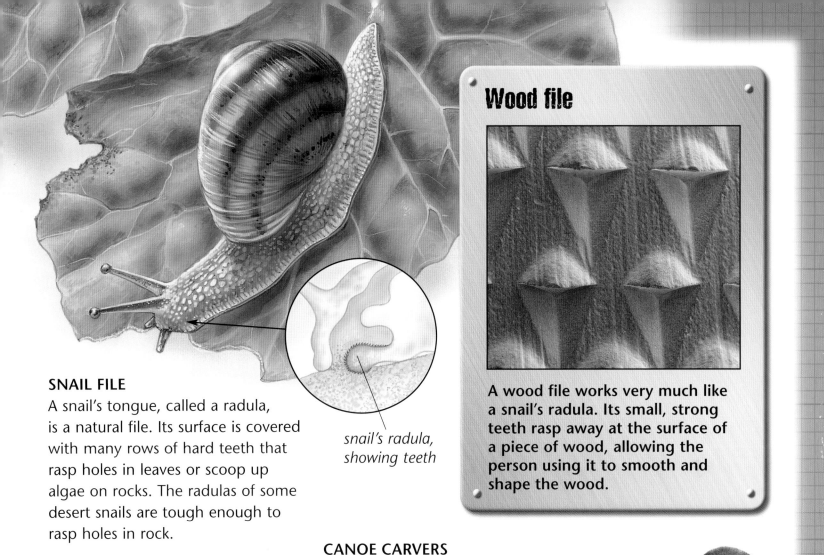

Wood file

A wood file works very much like a snail's radula. Its small, strong teeth rasp away at the surface of a piece of wood, allowing the person using it to smooth and shape the wood.

SNAIL FILE

A snail's tongue, called a radula, is a natural file. Its surface is covered with many rows of hard teeth that rasp holes in leaves or scoop up algae on rocks. The radulas of some desert snails are tough enough to rasp holes in rock.

snail's radula, showing teeth

BEAVERING AWAY

The large incisor teeth of a beaver are ideal for cutting and shaping logs. They are still in perfect condition after almost 20 years of constant chewing and tree felling. The teeth grow continuously from the base to make up for wear. They are also self-sharpening, thanks to differences in the hardness of the tooth layers, which wear at different rates to leave a sharp edge.

CANOE CARVERS

Humans use tools shaped like a beaver's teeth to carve objects, such as canoes, out of wood. Unlike beavers' teeth, however, they soon wear out and become blunt. This means people regularly have to stop and sharpen the cutting edge of the blade.

incisor

blade

beaver skull

Gathering and collecting

Sorting objects into different sizes is an important step in many processes. In mining, coal and mineral ores are broken up and graded into different sizes for specific uses. In the food industry, vegetables are graded by size before they are sold. In most cases the easiest way to carry out the grading processes has been to copy nature, either by passing the objects through nets, grids, and meshes of different sizes or by passing them through finer and finer combs.

BEATING HAIRS

Mussels use a form of biological conveyor belt system for collecting food. The two halves of the shell open when the tide comes in and seawater covers the mussel. Tens of thousands of microscopic beating hairs, called cilia, create a current of water. The seawater contains minute food particles, which are trapped in sticky mucous that the mussel secretes over its cilia surface. The beating cilia then waft the food into the gut for digestion.

CONVEYOR BELTS

Conveyor belts are used in most factory production line systems. They look like giant rubber bands that run along rollers and carry a steady stream of parts to a point where they can be processed. Some airports have moving walkways for passengers, who stand on a conveyor belt that takes them to their departure point.

Sieves

Sieves, fishing nets, and whale jaws all work on the same principle, separating objects or particles of different sizes by passing them through a grid or mesh. Large particles stay on one side of the mesh, while smaller ones pass through.

BLUE WHALE

The blue whale, which is the world's largest animal, is a baleen whale. It feeds by filtering small shrimplike animals called krill from the seawater. Its mouth is filled with rows of baleen (whalebone) plates, which act as a fine sieve and trap the krill.

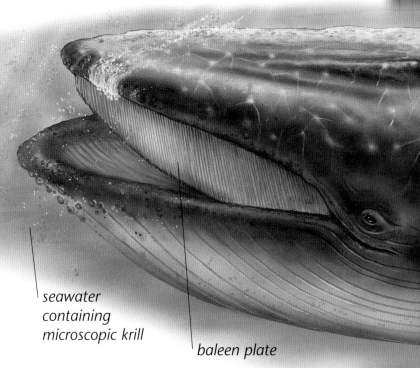

seawater containing microscopic krill

baleen plate

BUSY BODIES

Bees' bodies become dusted with pollen when they visit flowers. Their hind legs are equipped with combs that concentrate the pollen into a sticky ball in their pollen baskets. The pollen is then used as food for their larvae in the hive.

Collecting pollen

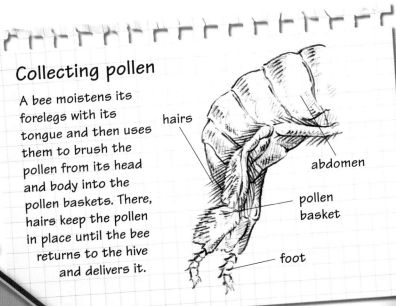

A bee moistens its forelegs with its tongue and then uses them to brush the pollen from its head and body into the pollen baskets. There, hairs keep the pollen in place until the bee returns to the hive and delivers it.

hairs

abdomen

pollen basket

foot

comb

pollen ball

Pincers and tweezers

✂ Toothed jaws and birds' beaks may have provided inspiration for the invention of scissors, which are now used for everything from slicing through metal plates to fine microsurgery in hospital operations. Objects cut into small pieces need to be picked up, and human fingers are often not delicate enough for this task. Again, the natural tools used by animals have provided a solution. Fine tweezers and probes are little more than copies of the devices found on many small animals' legs.

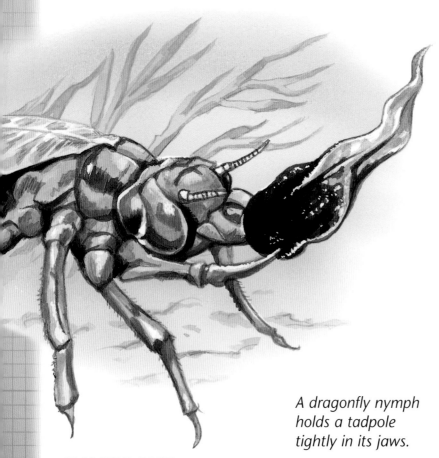

A dragonfly nymph holds a tadpole tightly in its jaws.

LIFTING TIMBER
The jaws of a timber-lifting device hold a whole tree trunk in the same way that a bird's beak holds a twig for use in building a nest. Instead of muscles, which a bird uses to open and close its beak, the jaws of a timber lifter are controlled by hydraulic power, using pressure to force liquid along narrow pipes.

CLAMPED FAST
The jaws of a dragonfly nymph are attached to the end of a hinged structure that is normally folded beneath its head. The jaws extend with lightning speed when prey comes within reach, impaling the body between the needle-sharp points of the jaw.

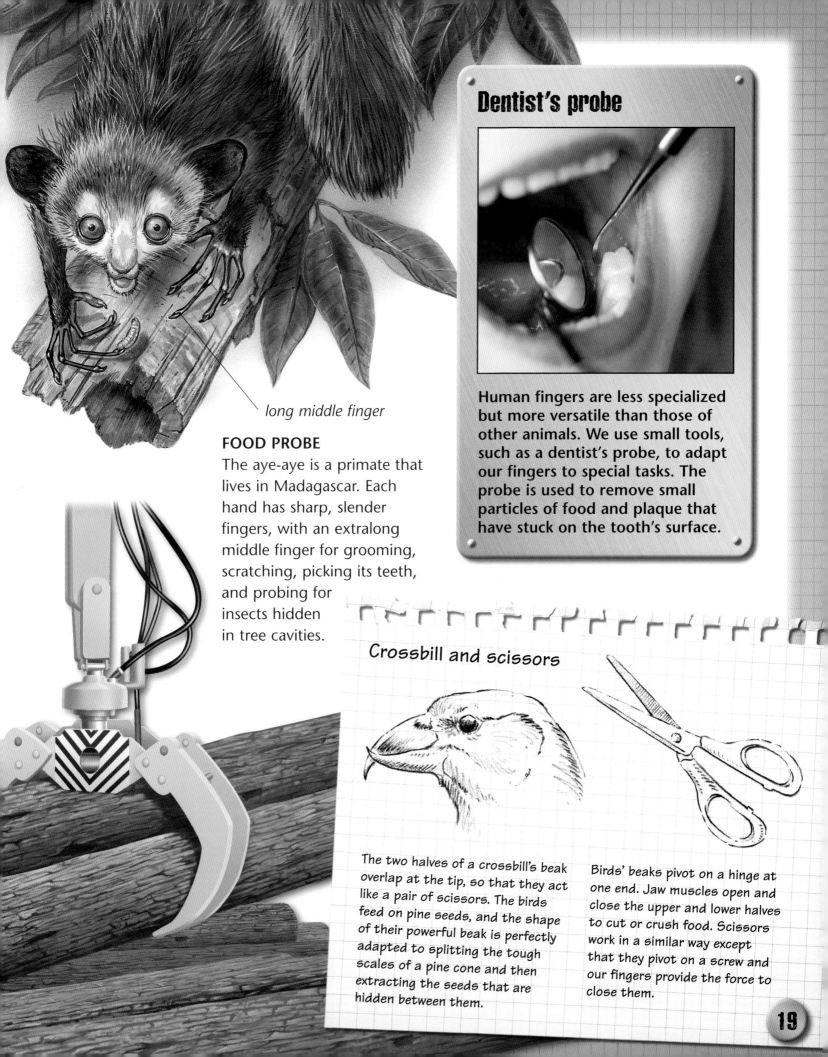

long middle finger

FOOD PROBE

The aye-aye is a primate that lives in Madagascar. Each hand has sharp, slender fingers, with an extralong middle finger for grooming, scratching, picking its teeth, and probing for insects hidden in tree cavities.

Dentist's probe

Human fingers are less specialized but more versatile than those of other animals. We use small tools, such as a dentist's probe, to adapt our fingers to special tasks. The probe is used to remove small particles of food and plaque that have stuck on the tooth's surface.

Crossbill and scissors

The two halves of a crossbill's beak overlap at the tip, so that they act like a pair of scissors. The birds feed on pine seeds, and the shape of their powerful beak is perfectly adapted to splitting the tough scales of a pine cone and then extracting the seeds that are hidden between them.

Birds' beaks pivot on a hinge at one end. Jaw muscles open and close the upper and lower halves to cut or crush food. Scissors work in a similar way except that they pivot on a screw and our fingers provide the force to close them.

Warmth

 Our bodies generate heat energy when we digest food, and one of the best ways to keep warm is to stop that heat from escaping too quickly. We can do this by wearing extra layers of clothes, so that each layer traps another layer of warm air. This way of preventing energy loss is called insulation.

COOL SHADES
Desert animals have a different problem. They must prevent themselves from overheating. Horned lizards can change the color of their skin to maintain a stable body temperature. In the morning, when they are cold and the sun is low in the sky, their skin is dark and absorbs heat. By midday, when the sun is hottest, their skin becomes pale, so that it reflects the sun's heat.

FUR LAYERS
Polar bears have different layers of fur to insulate them in the cold Arctic climate. The fur of the outer layer is clear and hollow and allows them to absorb the sun's warmth. Finer hairs close to the skin trap the warm air. The fur also keeps the bears' skin dry.

CLOTHING LAYERS
The layers in the clothes that Arctic explorers wear do different jobs. The inner layers trap heat close to the skin, while the outer layers draw moisture away from the skin to limit dampness and further heat loss.

outer coat layer

three inner coat layers

woolen sweater

thermal undershirt

skin

downy chest feathers

A COZY NEST

Birds' feathers keep them warm as well as enabling them to fly. Eider ducks, like most birds, sit on their eggs to keep them warm and ensure that they hatch. They also use their soft, downy chest feathers to line their nests and keep the eggs and young warm. Eider down is one of the best natural insulators, trapping layers of warm air.

heat-shielding tiles

SPACE SHUTTLE

Earth's atmosphere absorbs some of the energy from the sun before it reaches the ground. Spacecraft in orbit above the atmosphere are exposed to intense sunlight, but the white tiles that shield them from heat when they reenter the atmosphere also reflect away the sun's rays while they are in orbit, reducing heat absorption.

Keeping warm at night

A comforter keeps you warm while you are asleep because it is filled with insulating materials that trap layers of warm air. This insulation slows down the loss of heat from the body. Some comforters are filled with down feathers from birds, but many now contain special human-made fibers that have the same properties but are easier to clean.

Blood circulation in wading birds

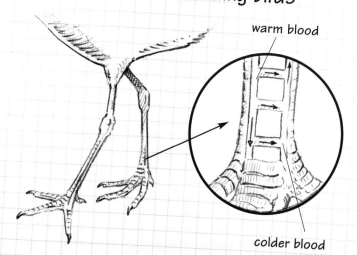

warm blood

colder blood

Wading birds, with their feet in cold water or on ice, have a specially adapted blood system in their legs that reduces heat loss. The blood vessels run close together, so the downward-flowing warm blood warms the upward-flowing cold blood. This also reduces the shock of very cold blood arriving back in the body from the feet. This heat exchange system is similar to those used in some human-made machines.

Blood flowing back to the body is kept warm by the vessels containing the blood flowing down to the feet.

Fungus and compost

Rotting plant material produces heat. When plants die, they are broken down by fungi and bacteria that digest and use the remains for their own growth. This process of digestion releases heat energy. If the plant material is piled in a heap, the heat is trapped inside in a process called composting. Some animals exploit this natural system to keep their eggs warm.

COMPOST BINS

Gardeners often build compost heaps to provide rich decayed plant material to spread on their soil. Compost heaps need to be constructed from layers of plant material with different textures, allowing oxygen to reach the fungi and bacteria that attack the dead plants. When decay begins, the heap warms up and the rotting process speeds up. But if the heap becomes too hot, the bacteria and fungi are killed. The warmth also attracts cold-blooded animals, such as snakes and frogs.

heat rising

lid

compost

fungi

bin

grass snake

hatch

slow worm

hibernating frog

Leaf-cutter ants' nest

The nests of leaf-cutter ants have different chambers for different purposes.

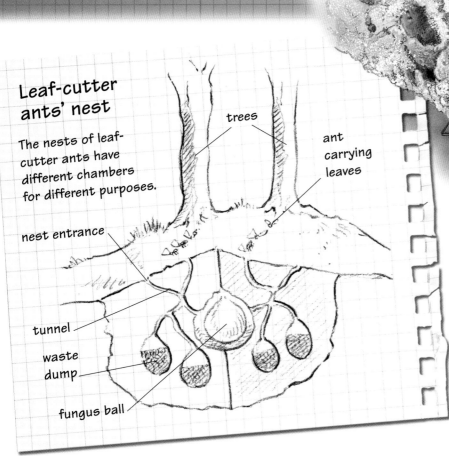

trees

ant carrying leaves

nest entrance

tunnel

waste dump

fungus ball

FUNGUS GARDENS

Fungi provide a nutritious food source for many small animals. Leaf-cutter ants make their own compost heaps, cultivating fungus gardens in their underground nests. The ants cut out and carry pieces of leaves into special chambers in their nests, where the pieces are allowed to rot. The fungi that grow on the surfaces of the leaves then become a useful source of food for the ants.

MALLEE FOWL

Mallee fowl cover their eggs with a warm layer of decaying vegetation, which incubates their eggs. They cover this compost heap with sand. If the eggs become too warm, they scrape sand away, letting heat energy escape.

sand

compost

eggs

Artificial incubation

Farmers often hatch eggs in artificial incubators. Without a parent for warmth, eggs (and then chicks) are warmed by heat from special light bulbs, keeping them at the perfect temperature to ensure that they hatch and thrive.

Absorbing energy

Catching prey, or escaping predators, can depend on fast movement. But the shock of such movement can be damaging unless the energy—called kinetic energy—is absorbed when the animal stops suddenly. Natural systems have evolved to absorb kinetic energy, protecting organs and tissues. People who travel at high speed depend on similar solutions to protect them, too.

AIRCRAFT CARRIERS

On an aircraft carrier, an airplane has only a short distance on which to land. Special arrestor wires, stretched across the deck, bring the plane to a safe halt. The extending wire absorbs its kinetic energy, just as the thread of a spider web cushions the impact of a colliding fly.

FLY TRAP

A spider web is covered with a liquid secreted by the spider. Surface tension draws this into tiny droplets, each of which pulls in a coil of silk. When a fly collides with the web, the impact is absorbed by the silk in the droplets, which is reeled out so that the thread gets longer without breaking.

uncoiled silk

coiled silk

Plane lowers hook ready to pick up the arrestor wire.

Arrestor wires move smoothly around pulley wheels.

SOFTENING THE BLOW

Many animals need to protect their brains from damage. The brain of a bighorn ram is protected by a bony shield, called an ossicone, which absorbs the energy from blows when it head butts another ram during a fight. A bicyclist's safety helmet uses a similar system of energy absorption, preventing skull fractures and brain damage in a collision.

bighorn ram

bicycle helmet

How does it work?

Mattress springs are coiled like the tendrils of a climbing plant. They absorb the weight and movement of your body, providing a comfortable surface to sleep on.

tendril

TENDRILS

As soon as the tendrils of climbing plants, such as vines, pea plants, or this passionflower, touch an object, they begin to coil around it. Once attached, the tendril coils into a spring, which acts as a natural shock absorber when the plant is buffeted by the wind.

Arrestor wire absorbs the kinetic energy and brings the plane to a halt.

Hook picks up arrestor wire, which stretches with the force of the plane's kinetic energy.

Woodpecker skull

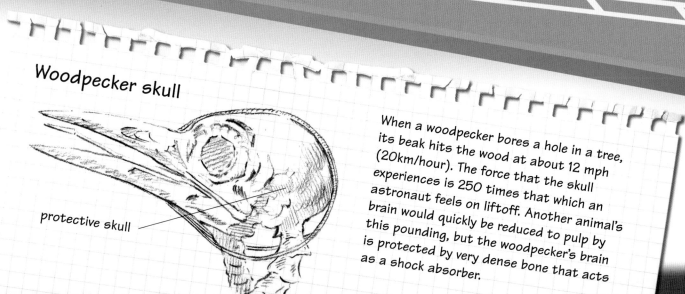

protective skull

When a woodpecker bores a hole in a tree, its beak hits the wood at about 12 mph (20km/hour). The force that the skull experiences is 250 times that which an astronaut feels on liftoff. Another animal's brain would quickly be reduced to pulp by this pounding, but the woodpecker's brain is protected by very dense bone that acts as a shock absorber.

Stored energy

Materials contain stored energy, which is also called potential energy because it has the potential to be converted into other forms of energy, such as light and heat. We burn coal, oil, and gas to convert their chemical energy into heat and to generate electricity.

POLE VAULTERS

The kinetic energy generated during a pole vaulter's sprint is converted to potential energy when the pole touches the ground. The pole bends, and when its natural elasticity begins to straighten it, it releases energy and hurls the vaulter over the bar.

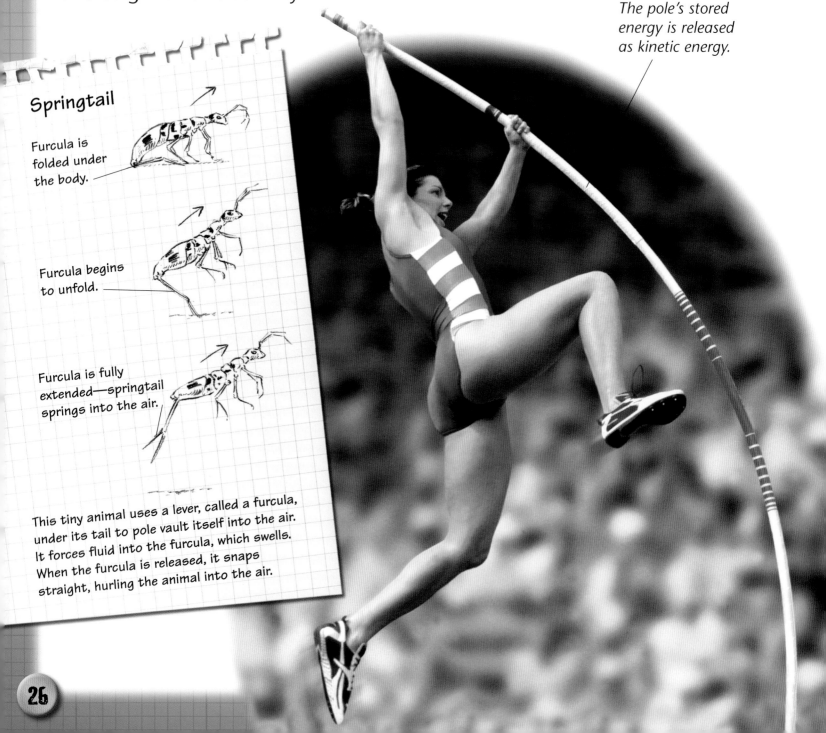

The pole's stored energy is released as kinetic energy.

Springtail

Furcula is folded under the body.

Furcula begins to unfold.

Furcula is fully extended—springtail springs into the air.

This tiny animal uses a lever, called a furcula, under its tail to pole vault itself into the air. It forces fluid into the furcula, which swells. When the furcula is released, it snaps straight, hurling the animal into the air.

Defibrillator

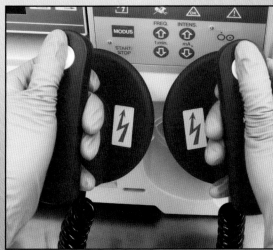

A defibrillator uses stored electricity to restart a heart that has stopped beating. The sudden electric charge that is released shocks the muscles of the heart into working again and can save a person's life.

MARATHON RUNNERS

Marathon runners pack their bodies with stored energy before a race. They eat very little for a few days and then consume lots of starchy foods. This makes their muscles store extra glycogen, a carbohydrate that provides the chemical energy that powers their muscles.

ELECTRIC EELS

Electric eels can carry a charge of up to 600 volts, which can stun a fish or even a person. Layers of muscle in its body act like the plates of a storage battery, accumulating an electric charge that the fish can release suddenly.

CARBOHYDRATES

Carbohydrates are more easily converted into energy than either proteins or fats, so they are a great form of stored energy. There are two types of carbohydrate foods. Complex carbohydrates, also known as starches, provide energy for longer than simple carbohydrates, or sugars, so are better for sustained activity, such as marathon running.

Foods high in complex carbohydrates include bread, rice, and pasta.

Glycogen granules are stored between muscle fibers. They are broken down to release energy for muscle contraction during exercise.

Hydraulics

✦ Hydraulic forces are used in animals for two main purposes. Some invertebrates have a hydrostatic skeleton, where the fluid inside their body cavity controls their shape. Their body changes shape when muscles force fluid from one area to another. Hydraulic forces also move liquids around the body inside tubes. Our hearts, for example, pump blood around our bodies.

Principles of hydraulics

When force is applied to a liquid inside a rigid container, its volume does not get smaller. Instead, the force is transmitted through the liquid. A small volume of liquid, pumped through a narrow pipe, carries enough force to move a large object a short distance, as shown in the diagram here.

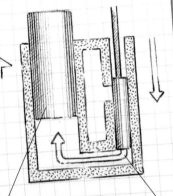

object moves up   liquid forced down

ELEVATORS

In an elevator, hydraulic pressure is transmitted through small pipes. Fluid is pumped into the bottom of the cylinder to push the elevator up. The fluid is then pumped out to move the elevator down. Hydraulic forces are also used in jacks, which lift cars and trucks so that wheels can be removed. Hydraulic crushers can transmit enough force to squeeze a scrap car into a solid block of metal.

EARTHWORMS

An earthworm uses hydraulic pressure to move inside a burrow. Muscles at the tail end contract, making it fatter and anchoring it against the soil. Then muscles at the head end contract, making the head end swell, and the worm shortens, drawing the tail toward the head, ready to repeat the whole cycle.

leaves with high turgor pressure

leaves with low turgor pressure

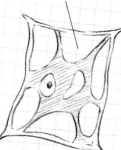

Turgor pressure

high pressure

low pressure

Leaves are held in shape by turgor pressure, a hydraulic force that pushes against the wall of every cell. When this force decreases, the cells collapse and the leaves wilt.

THIRSTY PLANTS

When the soil around a plant becomes too dry, the plant begins to dry up, too. The pressure inside the leaves falls, and they collapse.

starfish tube feet

Starfish feet

Starfish have a hydrostatic skeleton and rows of tube-shaped feet spaced regularly along each arm. These are connected to internal pipes filled with fluid. Hydraulic pressure forces fluid into the feet when muscles squeeze the pipes. A starfish creeps forward by extending, bending, and retracting the feet in sequence, using waves of muscle-driven hydraulic power.

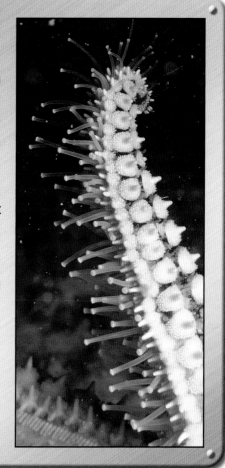

Gliding and sailing

wings made of fiberglass

Flight first evolved in insects, which beat their wings rapidly using powerful muscles. Some midges (small flys) beat their wings up to 1,000 times a second. This system uses too much energy to lift large animals off the ground. Aircraft exploit a less energetic principle that evolved separately in birds and that depends on the aerodynamics of curved wing surfaces. Air flows faster over the longer, curved top of the wing, creating an area of low pressure. This causes the wing to move upward and is the force we call lift.

PARACHUTISTS

Human parachutists use the same principle as plant seeds: air that is trapped under the parachute canopy creates drag and slows their fall. Modern parachutes can also be flown like a glider and steered by spilling air from parts of the canopy.

WING SKINS

Wings on the earliest airplanes were made from fabric skin that was stretched across a light framework, mimicking the construction of the wings of extinct pterodactyls.

DANDELIONS

Drag, or air resistance, slows falling objects, in addition to slowing aircraft down as they move forward. Plants have used parachutes that exploit this effect to spread their seeds for millions of years. The dandelion's plume of hairs slows its fall, so the wind carries the seed farther away from the parent plant. Rising currents of warm air even carry plumed seeds upward, which explains how dandelions come to grow on the tops of tall buildings.

albatross

GLIDING BIRDS

Long, narrow wings like those of an albatross produce less drag as they move through the air, so they are ideal for gliding birds. Human-made gliders use the same principle, and they can travel long distances without engines or any other mechanical source of energy.

GLIDERS

Gliders do not have engines. They can fly only if they are towed up into the air. The forward speed of a glider's wings generates lift, but glider pilots also look for columns of rising warm air, called thermals, to provide some of the lift that keeps their craft airborne. This technique is also used by soaring eagles, which can reach high altitudes by riding on thermals.

Sailing boats

Sails have an airfoil shape and behave like vertical wings. When a boat is sailing into the wind, it is driven forward by differences in air pressure on opposite sides of the sail.

JELLYFISH

Velella velella, the by-the-wind sailor, is a jellyfish that floats just below the ocean's surface. It is carried wherever the wind blows by its vertical sail, which is held above the surface of the water.

sail

Rudders

Puffins use both their tails and feet as rudders to steer them and also as brakes to slow them down.

feet

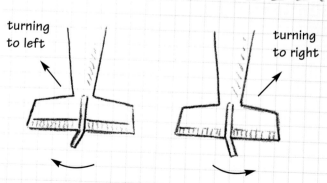

turning to left

turning to right

Aircraft have movable surfaces on their wings and tail that are used to change the direction of the flow of air so that they can turn or move up and down. The hinged surfaces are rigid and less maneuverable than the flexible tail of a bird.

Jet propulsion

 Jet propulsion works by forcing gas or liquid under high pressure through a small nozzle so that the fluid pushes against surrounding air or liquid, driving the container forward.

SQUIDS

Squids use jet propulsion to drive themselves through the ocean. A squid's body contains a powerful elastic bag of contracting muscles that squeeze a jet of water out of a backward-pointing nozzle. The animal swims up to 20 mph (32km/hour) when escaping from predators, sometimes even leaping out of the water and onto the deck of a ship.

nozzle

spores

PUFFBALLS

Puffball toadstools consist of a thin spherical skin packed with dustlike spores that can each grow into a new organism. Raindrops falling on the skin force a jet of air out through a small hole in the top of the fungus. This jet of air carries with it a cloud of spores.

HARRIER JUMP JETS

A jet engine sucks in air at one end and forces it out of the other at a much greater speed. Vertical takeoff aircraft, like the Harrier, use jet engines with nozzles that direct the high-pressure exhaust from the engines downward for takeoff. They swivel to point backward when the plane is airborne, so it flies forward.

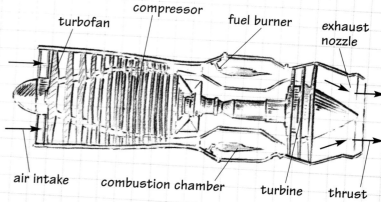

Jet engine

turbofan · compressor · fuel burner · exhaust nozzle

air intake · combustion chamber · turbine · thrust

The flow of air in the engine of a jet-powered vehicle moves from front to back, driving the vehicle in the opposite direction. The spinning turbofan sucks air into the combustion chamber, where it is compressed, mixed with fuel, and ignited. The expanding gases drive the turbine blades. These are linked via a shaft to the turbofan blades that suck air into the engine at the front. The hot escaping gases from the exhaust generate the thrust that moves the vehicle forward.

SQUIRTING CUCUMBERS

The squirting cucumber grows alongside roads in southern Europe and disperses its seeds in a jet of liquid. Water pressure builds up in the balloon-shaped fruit, which separates suddenly from its stalk. Then the seeds are squirted out in a jet of sticky liquid.

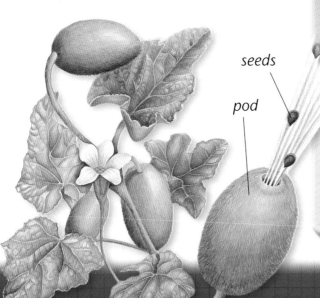

seeds

pod

Roman candles

People also use jet propulsion to propel objects out of containers. Jet engines force air into a chamber where fuel is burned, producing hot gases that shoot out and thrust the vehicle forward. Many fireworks, such as Roman candles, are also blasted into the air by a jet of hot gas. Explosives ignite in the tube, and the glowing balls of burning chemicals are shot out of the tube, propelled by expanding hot gases. Different chemicals produce different colors.

Floating and buoyancy

Objects float only if they are less dense than water. Then, the volume of water that they displace (push aside) weighs more than they do and pushes back with enough force to keep them afloat. Objects that are denser than water are heavier than the volume of water they displace, so they sink. Dense, heavy objects can be made to float if bubbles of air are trapped inside them. Ships sink when water replaces the air inside their hulls.

NAUTILUS

The nautilus is a primitive marine mollusk that is related to squids and octopuses. Unlike these animals, it has a shell that is divided into a spiral series of buoyancy chambers. The animal lives in the outermost chamber. It fills the others with just enough gas to match its overall density with that of the surrounding seawater, so that it neither sinks nor floats upward.

gas chambers inside the shell

living chamber

SUBMARINES

Submarines need to be able to float on the surface and dive beneath it. Compartments filled with air in a submarine's hull serve the same purpose as the nautilus's buoyancy chambers. The density of seawater increases in the deeper ocean, so a submarine's crew alters its buoyancy by pumping water in or out, to match the density of the seawater.

ballast tank

NAUTILUS CHAMBERS

A large nautilus shell contains about 30 buoyancy chambers. Extra chambers are added as the animal grows, to allow for its increased weight.

How does it work?

A submarine floats because the air inside it makes it less dense than the water it displaces. It can dive when water is pumped into ballast tanks to increase its density. To make it rise again, air is pumped in to replace the water.

ballast tanks filling

ballast tanks emptying

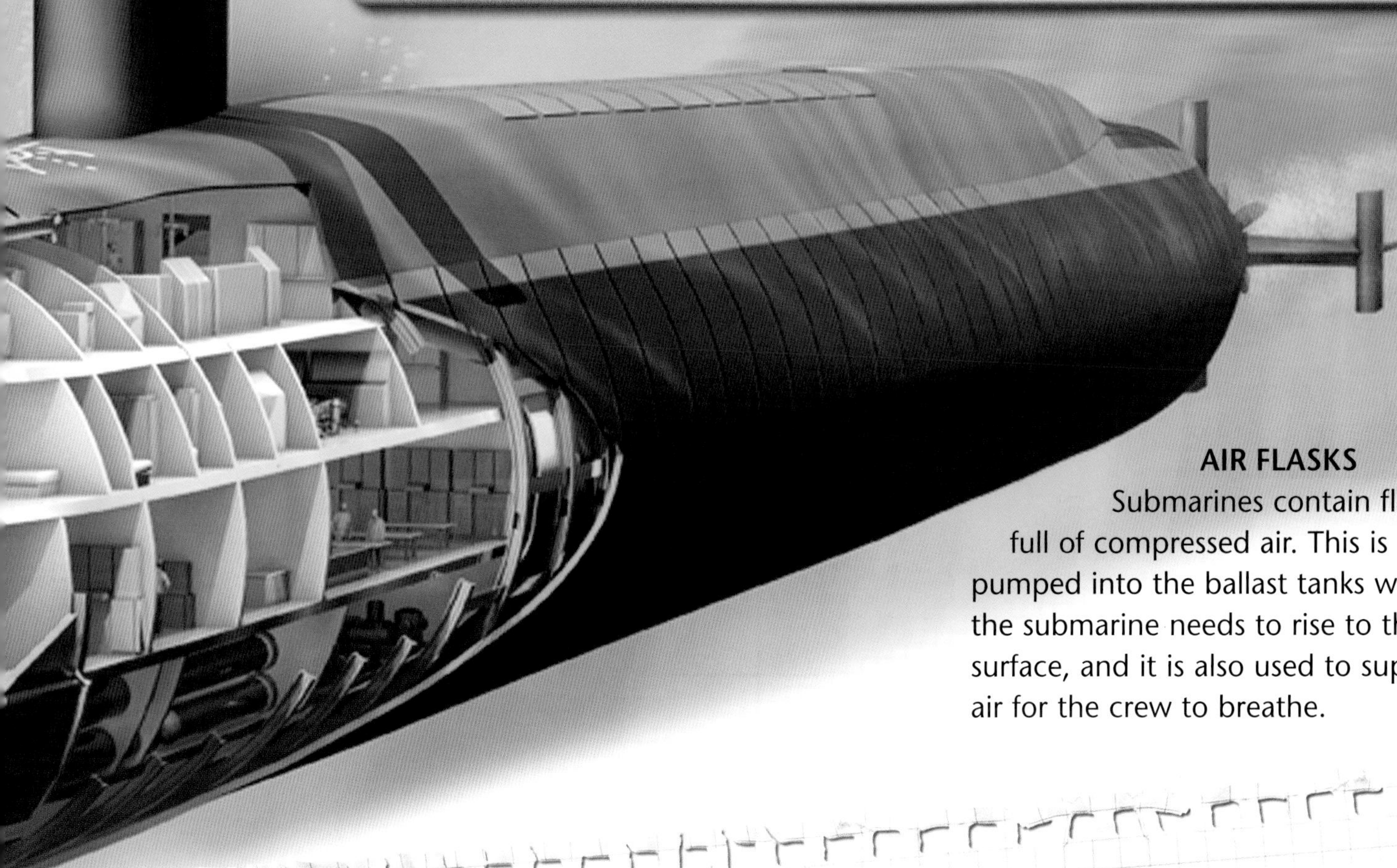

AIR FLASKS

Submarines contain flasks full of compressed air. This is pumped into the ballast tanks when the submarine needs to rise to the surface, and it is also used to supply air for the crew to breathe.

Fish's swim bladder

Many fish can control their density. By varying the amount of air in the swim bladder inside their body, they change their buoyancy so that it exactly balances their weight. Then they can float below the surface without rising or falling. Fish such as sharks, which do not have swim bladders, must swim constantly to prevent themselves from sinking.

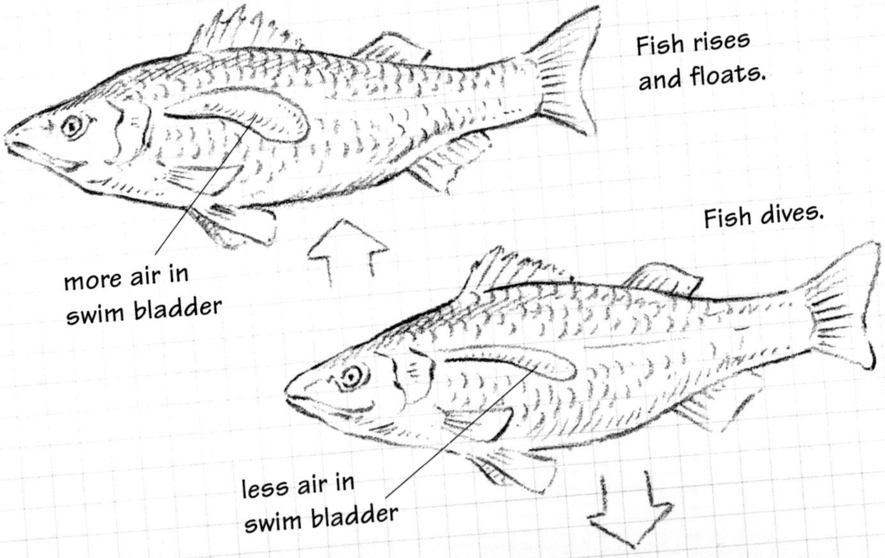

Fish rises and floats.

Fish dives.

more air in swim bladder

less air in swim bladder

Defense

Thick, heavy armor can protect animals and people from attack, but it can make its owner slow and clumsy. Large sheets of rigid armor also restrict movement and, in more mobile animals, are replaced by systems of small, overlapping plates or scales, which provide flexible protection. Many animals have evolved armor that covers only their most vulnerable parts. The disadvantage of being less well protected is balanced by the advantage of being lighter and able to move more easily.

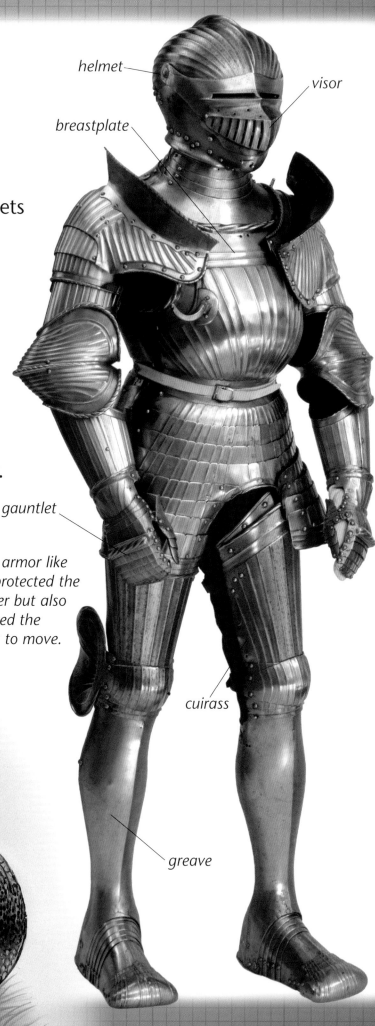

helmet

visor

breastplate

gauntlet

Plate armor like this protected the wearer but also allowed the joints to move.

cuirass

greave

An armadillo can quickly roll up into a tight ball inside its armored covering.

ARMADILLOS

Overlapping armored plates of bone, connected by softer skin, protect the back of an armadillo. These provide enough flexibility for the animal to move fast and easily. When the animal is attacked, its flexible armor allows it to roll up, protecting its soft underparts, head, and legs inside a ball of armor plate.

Shooting spines

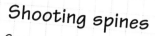

Sea anemones can fire needle-sharp spines into their attackers. The anemone's tentacles are covered with tiny cells called nematocysts, which contain coiled, barbed threads that shoot out with lightning speed when another animal brushes against their surface. When triggered, the nematocysts turn inside out to reveal their spines.

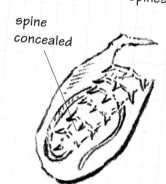

spine concealed

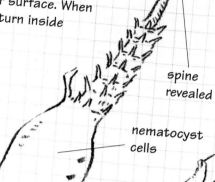

spine revealed

nematocyst cells

Harpoons

A harpoon works much like the spines of a sea anemone. A gun fires the weapon, which is like a small spear and is attached to a line. This can then be used to pull the fish or other animal in, and it can be retrieved to be used again.

spear

harpoon gun

trigger

Razor wire

Barbed wire was originally designed to make quick, cheap fences that would stop domestic animals from wandering away. It has the same effect as a barrier of thorny roses or a briar patch. Barbed wire is now also used to protect buildings against intruders, trapping anyone who tries to push their way through its razor-covered coils and wounding them.

BRIAR PATCHES

Plants cannot run away from their enemies, so they often use spines to deter grazing animals that would otherwise eat them. If the stems of thorny plants are cut down, the new growth that replaces them often develops an even denser covering of spines, increasing protection against future attack. Thorns are usually formed from modified leaves that have become woody and sharp.

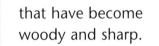

Smoke screens and alarms

Mechanical defenses, such as armor and spines, can be very effective but can also hinder their user. Chemical defenses are compact and far more convenient because they are used only when their owner is actually attacked. They can usually be replaced quickly, unlike damaged mechanical defenses. Animals' chemical deterrents are so effective that they have been copied by humans—police forces sometimes quell riots by spraying the rioters with irritant chemicals, such as tear gas, and in some places people may carry special chemical sprays to defend themselves from attack.

ink

INK CLOUD
Sometimes chemical defenses can create confusion. Octopuses and cuttlefish have ink sacs full of dye. If they are attacked, they squirt a cloud of dye into the water and then quickly escape, hidden from enemies by their chemical smoke screen.

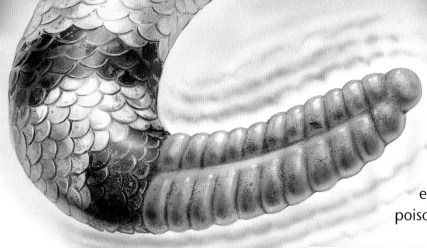

SOUNDING THE ALARM

Rattlesnakes are well camouflaged and risk being accidentally stepped on by large animals. If an animal gets too close, the snake shakes a loud rattle on its tail, which frightens the intruder away. This alarm ensures that the snake does not waste its poisonous bite on an animal too large to eat.

UNDER COVER

In wartime, the element of surprise is very important, so soldiers may move into battle under cover of a dense smoke screen.

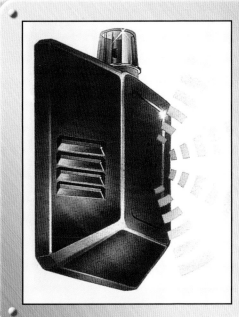

Burglar alarms

Often people protect their homes from burglars by using loud alarm bells. Hidden switches inside the house set off the alarm if someone enters and may automatically alert the police. The alarm is often visible outside the house, which should deter burglars from targeting it.

Bombardier beetle

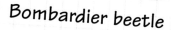
boiling liquid

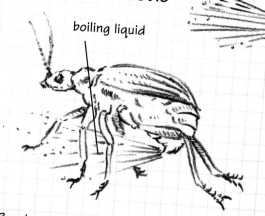

Bombardier beetles repel enemies by firing boiling chemicals from their tails. Any animal that seizes the beetle drops it instantly. Once when the naturalist Charles Darwin was collecting beetles, he put a bombardier beetle in his mouth because his hands were full. The intense pain took him by surprise!

Hand-held spray cans use a mechanism similar to the bombardier beetle's.

Camouflage and warning signs

☢ Color can be used as a method of defense, to warn or to hide. If an animal is poisonous and can bite and sting, then bright colors can act as a warning to potential enemies that they may be injured or killed if they get too close. Predators soon learn to associate certain easily recognized color schemes with danger. If an animal needs to hide from danger or conceal itself while on the lookout for prey, it often has colors that match its normal background, making it difficult to see. This is called camouflage.

FLOWER POWER
Flower mantises sit perfectly still among the flowers on plants. They are so well camouflaged that other insects mistake them for flower petals. Then, once the prey insect lands on the flower, the mantis grabs it.

ARMY CAMOUFLAGE
Armies use camouflage nets to hide their tanks and other vehicles from cameras in aircraft. The nets conceal the tank's sharp outlines and blend with the surrounding vegetation. Military vehicles are also usually painted in camouflage patterns to match the colors of the surrounding landscape.

POISON-ARROW FROGS

South American poison-arrow frogs produce some of the world's most deadly poisons in their skin. One animal carries enough poison to kill ten people. The bright colors of these little frogs serve as a constant warning to all other animals to leave them alone.

HAZARD SIGNS

The sign on the right is the international warning sign for a radioactive hazard, and it is displayed wherever dangerous radiation is emitted. It uses the same yellow and black colors as yellow jackets to warn of danger. Warning signs have to be visible and instantly recognized by all, no matter what language they speak. Signs such as the ones at right use colors that are widely understood to signify danger.

radioactivity

YELLOW JACKETS

Yellow jackets are armed with poisonous stingers. They also have characteristic black and yellow stripes, which act as a warning to other animals. These warning markings are common among animals, and many different species carry similar patterns and striking color combinations. Predators always associate these markings with danger, even if their owners are harmless. Hoverflies, for example, have no stinger, but they copy the colors of yellow jackets, and this similarity protects them.

explosives

flammable material

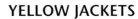

Sound and pressure waves

Sound and pressure wave systems for detecting underwater objects have developed rapidly since the early 20th century. This technology is an important military tool for submarine warfare, but it has many peaceful uses, too. Sonar has allowed the mapping of the sea floor. It can even be used to listen to the songs of whales.

ECHOLOCATION

Sound waves bounce off solid objects and send back echoes. Animals such as dolphins and bats use their ability to hear these echoes to locate and avoid hitting solid objects and to find prey animals in conditions that make it difficult to see them.

DOLPHINS

A dolphin's head contains a fatty organ called a melon, which focuses sound waves into a sonar beam. Dolphins hunt schools of fish by listening for echoes reflected from their prey.

sonar beam returning

sonar beam sent out

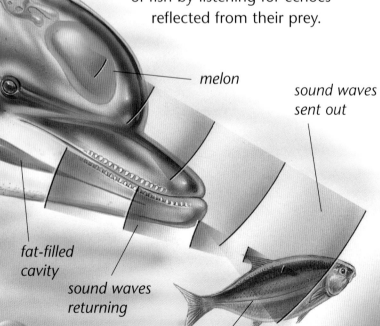

melon

sound waves sent out

fat-filled cavity

sound waves returning

fish

SONAR

Sonar stands for "SOund Navigation And Ranging." Active sonar involves generating a sound pulse and measuring the time taken for echoes from underwater objects to return. This allows their distance to be measured. Passive sonar does not send out sound waves but just listens to them. This system does not betray the presence of the listener.

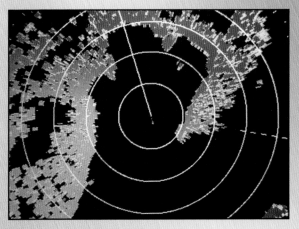

sound waves sent out

sound waves returning

ULTRASOUND

Some bats emit high-pitched ultrasound waves. These bounce back from any object that they hit, and as the bat closes in on prey, the returning sound waves increase in frequency. This allows the bat to judge the distance of its prey as the bat closes in and to navigate in dark caves. Several moth species can detect the bat's ultrasound and have evolved escape methods. Some drop to the ground as soon as they pick up the signals. Others confuse the bat's detection system by emitting high-pitched squeaks themselves.

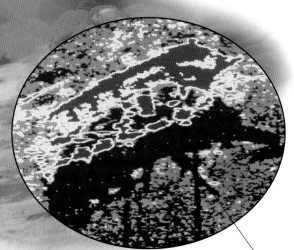

ultrasound photograph of shipwreck

Radar

Radar is a system that uses electromagnetic waves (radio or microwaves) in much the same way as sonar uses sound waves. *Radar* stands for "RAdio Detection And Ranging" and can obtain information about the direction, speed, and altitude (height) of both still and moving objects such as ships, aircraft, and even weather formations. Radar can operate at longer ranges than sonar.

Vibrations

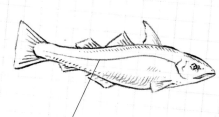

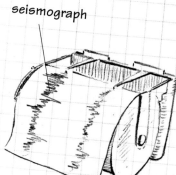

seismograph

lateral line

Some fish have a very sensitive system for detecting underwater movement. A lateral line canal along the sides of the fish contains sensitive hairs and is open through pores to the outside water. Water movements caused by pressure changes and vibrations rock the hairs and generate nerve signals. In this way, fish are aware of other animals nearby. We use mechanical vibration detectors, called seismographs, to detect earthquake tremors.

Light and heat sensing

Human eyes detect only certain kinds of light, which are found within the spectrum of a rainbow. These stretch from short-wavelength violet to long-wavelength red. Infrared cameras can detect warm objects (which emit longer-wavelength infrared light) in total darkness. Many cameras that protect buildings from intruders at night work on this principle.

SEEING LIGHT

Light enters our eyes through a narrow hole in the front called the pupil. A lens behind the pupil focuses light onto a layer of cells, called the retina, at the back of the eye. They receive the image (which is upside down) and convert it into electrical signals, which they send to the brain. The brain then makes sense of the signals, including turning the image the right way up. Eyes can adjust to changes in light intensity with the iris, which surrounds the pupil. The iris uses muscles to open or close the pupil in dim or bright light.

Iris diaphragm regulates light entering the camera.

Glass lens focuses light rays.

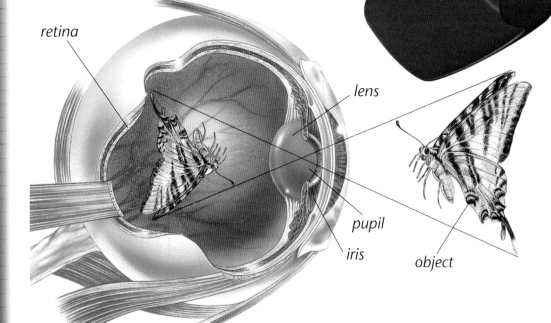

retina

lens

pupil

iris

object

DIGITAL CAMERA

Digital cameras are based on simple versions of our eyes. A lens focuses an image onto a sensor. This converts the light energy into electrical signals that are transferred to a memory card. An iris diaphragm acts like the pupil of an eye, controlling the amount of light that reaches the sensor.

Sensor converts light energy into an electrical charge.

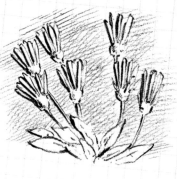

Some flowers are sensitive to changes in light intensity. Their petals close up at night and may even close when a dark cloud covers the sun. This behavior is thought to protect pollen from dew at night and from approaching rain during the day. We use sensors that detect light intensity changes as automatic switches, to turn street lights on in evening twilight and off at dawn.

PIT VIPER

Pit vipers are equipped with infrared sensors on either side of their jaws. These can form a thermal (heat) image of their prey in total darkness. Their victims are not aware that they are being hunted until it is too late to escape.

infrared sensor pits

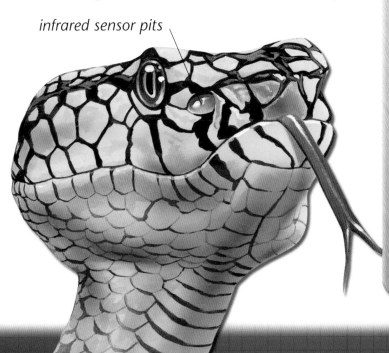

Infrared images

Warm bodies give off infrared radiation, which is invisible to the human eye. Infrared light can be detected by special cameras and films, which give false colors to the different strengths of radiation they record. As you can see, the center of this dog's body is warmer than its ears, feet, and cold nose.

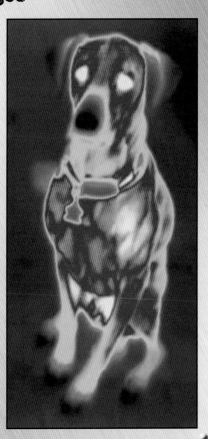

Magnetism and gravity

⌐ We use our planet's magnetic field to navigate our way around Earth's surface, to create accurate maps, and to plot travel routes between places. Exploring Earth and space depends on accurate instruments. Today we can travel thousands of miles by airplane and arrive at a precise destination with pinpoint accuracy.

COMPASS
Earth has an iron core that behaves like a bar magnet with its ends close to the North and South poles. This core creates a magnetic field around the planet. A magnetized iron needle that is free to turn will always point north or south along Earth's lines of magnetic force toward the North or South pole. This is a simple compass.

HOMING PIGEONS
Scientists have found that homing pigeons get lost if magnets are attached to their heads. The pigeons navigate by orienting themselves to Earth's magnetic field. They have a natural compass, a magnetic compound of iron oxide called magnetite, embedded in their necks.

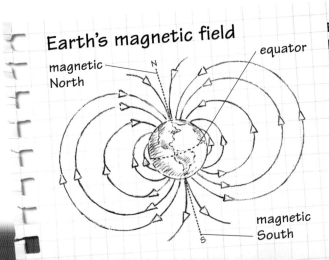

Earth's magnetic field

magnetic North

N

equator

magnetic South

S

Earth's magnetic field lies along an imaginary line between the North and South magnetic poles. However, these poles are constantly moving, so the magnetic field moves, too, by up to 9 mi. (15km) per year. The geographic North and South poles, however, are in fixed positions on Earth's surface.

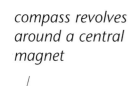

compass revolves around a central magnet

PLUMB LINE

A builder uses the effect of gravity on a plumb line (a weight on a fine cord) to help build vertical walls. Gravity pulls all objects directly toward the center of Earth, so the line is perpendicular to its surface.

weight

Toadstool gills

The closely spaced gills under a toadstool's cap are covered with spores, which drop down between the gills and are carried away by the wind. The gills keep perfectly vertical by detecting gravity, so that their spores can fall freely between them. If the toadstool is tilted, the gills quickly realign themselves.

METAL DETECTORS

Electrical fields can also be used to gather information. Metal detectors create electrical fields that penetrate the soil. Buried metal objects interact with the electrical field and send a signal to the operator's earphones.

electrical field

SHARKS

Sharks have special organs, called ampullae of Lorenzini, in their noses, which allow them to find prey that is completely hidden from view. These organs can detect the faint electrical signals produced by the twitching muscles of a fish buried below sand. The shark then blows away the sand and grabs the hiding fish.

ampullae of Lorenzini

prey

Light and electricity

💡 Light is a clean, free, endlessly renewable form of energy. Plants capture energy from sunlight with natural solar cells called chloroplasts. We store solar energy captured by solar cells as electricity in batteries.

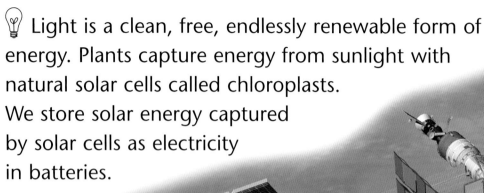

PHOTOSYNTHESIS

The cells of leaves are packed with chloroplasts, which contain chlorophyll. This chemical enables a reaction in which light energy breaks down water molecules, converting the energy into chemical energy (as well as producing sugar and oxygen) in a process called photosynthesis.

solar panel

SOLAR PANELS

A solar cell converts light into electrical energy. Each cell produces only a small amount of power, so large numbers of cells are needed. However, unlike stored energy sources such as oil, gas, or batteries, which eventually run out, solar cells will continue to produce power for as long as the sun shines on their surface. Scientists are working on ways to make solar panels more efficient.

light falling on surface of leaf

chloroplast

leaf cell

SPACE STATION

Solar panels are the best power source for instruments on spacecraft because the cells can provide power during flights that may last for many years. Batteries would be too heavy and would not last long enough to perform this task.

DEADLY SWITCH

Venus flytrap leaves catch flies when the insects touch trigger hairs on their surface. These act like electrical switches, triggering the flow of water out of cells along the leaf midrib, so that the leaf snaps shut.

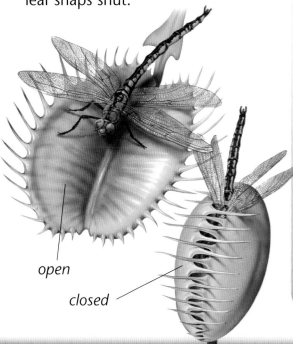

open

closed

Optical fibers

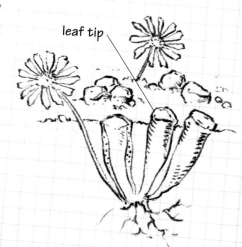

leaf tip

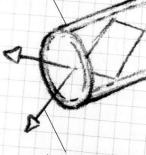

human-made optical fiber

light travels through tube

The fenestraria plant, which lives in the desert, uses optical fibers to allow it to photosynthesize. Fenestraria leaves are almost completely buried below the sand, which protects them from water loss and grazing animals. The tip of each leaf is transparent, so that light can enter and travel down the leaf, where photosynthesis takes place.

People have developed optical fibers of transparent glass covered with a material that acts as a mirror. Light beams are reflected down through the optical fibers' core. The fibers can be bent easily, so light can be shone around corners into awkward places. Fiber optics are used to carry coded messages in the form of pulses of light.

Electrical switch

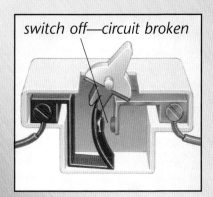

switch off—circuit broken

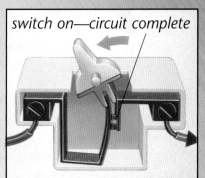

switch on—circuit complete

Electrical switches operate by breaking a circuit and stopping the flow of electric current through a wire. When the switch is turned on, the circuit is completed and electric current begins to flow through the wire again.

Gripping

Good grip is essential in everyday life for all land animals. We need grip to walk on surfaces where there is little friction or to handle smooth or wet objects. Grooved treads on shoes and tires, nonslip treads on the edges of stairs, and ribbed handles on tools and bicycle handlebars are all designed to provide a better grip.

HANGING ON

Limpets are mollusks that live on exposed seashores. They avoid being swept away by waves, or being dried out by the sun at low tide, by attaching themselves to rocks. They do this with a large, muscular foot that creates a powerful suction force, drawing the limpet down onto a rock's surface.

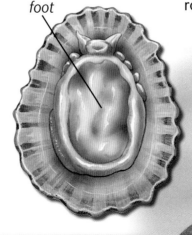

limpet's foot

RUNNING SHOES

Runners use spiked running shoes to give them a good grip on the track, in just the same way that the cheetah's claws help it grip the ground.

running shoe with spikes

SPIKED FEET

Cheetahs, which chase their prey at up to 60 mph (100km/hour), have long, permanently extended claws to help them grip loose surfaces.

cheetah's clawed paw

Fingerprints

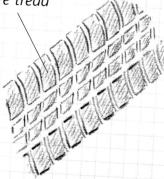

tire tread

Our fingers are covered with fine patterns of ridges and grooves, which help us grip smooth, slippery objects.

The tread pattern on a tire is a larger version of the same principle, designed to ensure that the tire grips wet roads.

limpet attached to rock

Suction cups

Suction cups are like mechanical limpets and are ideal for moving some awkward materials such as large plates of glass. The suction cup is elastic and will spring back when pushed onto a smooth surface. This creates a low-pressure area inside the cup because the edge is an airtight seal. Higher air pressure on the outside of the cup keeps it attached, unless the valve is opened to let the air pressures inside and outside become equal again, when the cup can be lifted off.

Fastenings

When we get dressed, we use a variety of temporary fastenings to keep our clothes in place. Laces, buckles, and buttons have been used for clothes and shoes for thousands of years, but two modern inventions—the zipper and Velcro—have made dressing faster and easier. Both inventions depend on joining objects with small hooks and draw inspiration from nature, where efficient flight in birds and the spreading of plant seeds both make use of the same technique.

barbules

ZIPPERS

A zipper uses a slide with wedges inside it to force the teeth apart or back together. The teeth are hooked so that they interlock to fasten securely, just like a bird's barbules.

teeth

BIRDS' FEATHERS

The flight feathers of birds generate lift when air flows over their surface. Each feather is made up of thousands of fine branches, called barbules, arranged along a central shaft. Every barbule has rows of microscopic hooks that interlock so that the feather has a flat, rigid surface.

BEES

Large flat wings are efficient but cannot be folded away easily for protection. Bees solve this problem by having two pairs of wings, joined by a row of fine hooks called a humulus. When the insect lands, the humulus is disconnected and the wings can be folded neatly along the bee's back.

humulus

wings

Velcro

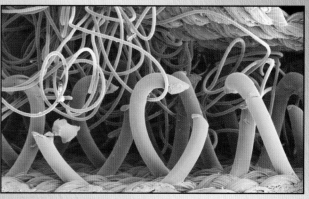

In 1957, George de Mestral, a Swiss engineer, found burs (hooked seed heads) clinging to his clothes and noticed their fine hooks. These inspired him to develop Velcro, a synthetic material made from two nylon strips. One strip is covered with tiny loops and the other coated with minute hooks. When pressed together, they stick firmly, but they can be instantly ripped apart.

BURS

A bur is a seed head covered with hundreds of small, sharp hooks. Burdock, a member of the thistle family, is one of many plants that shed their seeds in burs.

hooks of a bur

Surface protection

🐞 Surfaces need to be protected from water, grit, and even bright light. Polishing cars and furniture, oiling baseball gloves, and wearing ultraviolet-absorbing sunscreen are all ways of protecting surfaces. Animals and plants produce chemicals (secretions) in their cells, which they use to protect their surfaces.

SHOE LEATHER
Leather is made from cattle hide (skin). Natural oils are produced in the living animal's skin, keeping it supple and waterproof. Once the hide is made into a shoe, it dries, hardens, and loses its waterproofing. Grease is rubbed into leather to keep it both soft and waterproof.

waterproof leather surface

waterproof feathers

WATERPROOF FEATHERS
Ducks' feathers are coated with an oily secretion that prevents them from becoming waterlogged when the duck dives under the surface for food. The water droplets roll off the duck's back when it surfaces, keeping the feathers dry and the bird warm.

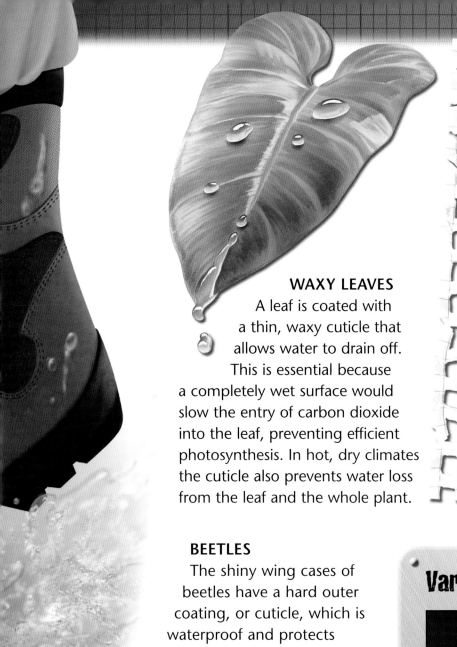

Natural glue

leaf attached to stem by pectin

pectin seals leaf scar when leaf drops off

Cells in plants are glued together with a natural adhesive called pectin. When leaves begin to fall from the trees in the autumn, an enzyme called pectinase is produced where the leaf stalk joins the twig. This dissolves the pectin glue, until eventually the leaf falls, leaving a scar that is protected by the remains of the pectin.

WAXY LEAVES

A leaf is coated with a thin, waxy cuticle that allows water to drain off. This is essential because a completely wet surface would slow the entry of carbon dioxide into the leaf, preventing efficient photosynthesis. In hot, dry climates the cuticle also prevents water loss from the leaf and the whole plant.

BEETLES

The shiny wing cases of beetles have a hard outer coating, or cuticle, which is waterproof and protects them from damage. The insect cuticle is reinforced with a protein called sclerotin, which makes it one of the toughest materials made by animals.

Varnished wood

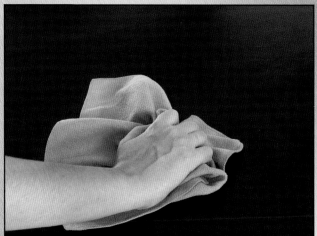

Varnishing or polishing wooden surfaces protects them from dirt, scratches, and water damage. Early varnishes, such as beeswax, were made from the natural oils and secretions of insects that used these substances for their own protection.

Liquids and lubricants

When we rub our hands together on a winter's day, we are using friction to generate heat. Friction between surfaces produces energy but also makes surfaces wear away. Friction is a constant problem for animals because it wears out their moving parts and because energy is needed to overcome friction between moving surfaces. Animals rely on lubricants to reduce wear and cut down the energy needed for movement. We use lubricants on moving parts in machines for the same reasons.

▼ *Oil levels must be checked regularly and topped up to keep a car's engine running smoothly.*

ENGINES

We reduce friction in machines by using oil or grease to lubricate their moving surfaces. If the oil levels in a car's engine and transmission are allowed to drop too far, friction between their rapidly moving parts will cause wear and overheating. Wheel bearings must also be greased, to reduce friction and allow free movement.

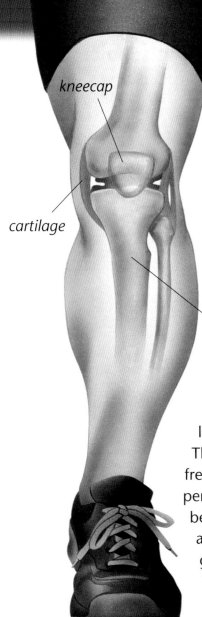

KNEE JOINTS

Joints between bones would soon wear out if they were not lubricated. Friction in joints such as the human knee is reduced by a covering of smooth cartilage on the joint surfaces, which are enclosed in a cavity filled with lubricating synovial fluid.

kneecap

cartilage

bone

ice crystals

TREE FROG

The American tree frog hibernates in the fallen leaves on forest floors. The frog can survive the freezing of up to 65 percent of its body water because it accumulates an antifreeze called glycerol in its blood. This prevents ice crystals from forming inside its delicate organs.

ICE CRYSTALS

When large ice crystals grow in cells, they kill them by bursting through the delicate cell membranes. Antifreezes can prevent ice formation, but other protective measures have also evolved. Some beetles can tolerate freezing because their blood contains special chemicals. These encourage the formation of minute ice crystals that are too small to damage their cells.

hibernating frog

Broken pipes

Antifreezes are added to car engines in the winter to prevent water from freezing in the cooling system. The expanding ice can split pipes, burst radiators, and damage engines.

Glossary

aerodynamic
Anything related to the flow of air over surfaces. An aerodynamic wing shape reduces the drag of air as it flows over the wing.

airfoil
Wings have curved surfaces above and below. This shape is called an airfoil and generates lift when air flows over it.

awn
A long, bristlelike structure found in cereals that works to plant the seed by gradually driving it into the ground.

axis
An imaginary line through an object that divides it into two halves.

bacteria
Tiny, single-celled organisms. Some bacteria cause disease, but many are useful because they break down and recycle dead organisms.

biodegradable
Something that can be broken down by bacteria and other living organisms.

buoyancy
The ability of an object to float.

camouflage
Colors, patterns, or shapes that make objects and living things difficult to see against their surroundings.

carbohydrate
A chemical compound of the elements carbon, hydrogen, and oxygen. Carbohydrates include sugars and starches. They are made by plants during photosynthesis and used to make plant cells and store energy in both plants and animals.

cartilage
Firm but flexible tissue, sometimes called gristle, found covering the end of joints and in the nose and ear.

characteristic
A feature or quality of a person, place, or thing. Particular characteristics enable us to recognize individuals and distinguish one object from another.

chlorophyll
A green compound in plant leaves used to capture energy from sunlight.

chloroplast
A tiny structure in a plant cell that contains chlorophyll.

civilization
An advanced stage in the development of humans as social beings. In civilized communities, people work for the good of the larger group as well as for themselves and their close family members.

cuticle
Skin or outer covering.

defibrillator
A machine that delivers an electric shock to the heart to allow it to resume normal beating.

density
The weight of a specific volume of a substace. A bag of coal is heavier than the same sized bag of feathers because coal is denser than feathers.

digestion
The breakdown of food into substances that can be absorbed by the body.

echolocation
The method of locating objects by sound reflected off their surfaces.

elastic
Able to bend or stretch when a force is applied. An elastic material returns to its original shape once the force is removed.

foliage
The leaves that cover a plant.

frequency
The number of times that something happens in a certain period. Sound travels as waves of energy. In high-frequency sound, many waves are produced in a short time.

friction
The resistance produced by one surface moving over another.

fungus
An organism, such as a mushroom, that has no leaves or flowers and reproduces by producing spores, not seeds.

gravity
The force that pulls objects together. The most obvious effect of gravity is to pull objects toward the center of Earth.

grubs
The young of some insects, such as ants. Also known as larvae.

hydraulic
Anything to do with liquid moving under pressure in a confined, or limited, space.

hydrostatic skeleton
The fluid that fills the hollow body cavity of animals such as worms and controls their shape.

incisor
A sharp-edged tooth at the front of the mouth, used for cutting.

incubation
The process by which an animal keeps its eggs warm in order for them to hatch. Most birds incubate their eggs by sitting on them in the nest.

insulation
A material that does not conduct heat, electricity, or sound.

invertebrate
An animal that does not have a backbone or internal skeleton. Some invertebrates have a hard outer covering, called an exoskeleton, instead.

kinetic energy
The energy in a moving body.

lubrication
Use of a fluid, such as grease or oil, to reduce friction and enable parts of the body or machinery to move smoothly.

membrane
A thin, skinlike material that covers, lines, or connects parts of the body.

mollusk
One of the main groups of invertebrates (animals without backbones). Snails, slugs, oysters, cuttlefish, octopuses, and squids are all mollusks.

mucous
A slimy substance produced by animals for protection or lubrication.

nutrient
Any one of a number of substances that are essential for the growth and survival of organisms.

nymph
An early stage in the development of some insects, such as dragonflies. Nymphs shed their skins several times before becoming adult insects.

organism
An individual animal, plant, or other life form.

photosynthesis
The process by which plants turn the energy from the sun into food.

pollen
The male cells of flowers, which must join with female egg cells before seeds can be formed.

potential energy
Energy that is stored in some way but can be released when needed.

predator
An animal that hunts other animals (the prey) for food.

prey
An animal that is hunted by other animals for food.

primate
One of a group of mammals including monkeys and apes. Human beings are classified as apes and therefore are part of this group.

radar
A system for detecting the position and speed of objects such as aircraft and ships by sending out radio waves in pulses, which are reflected off the object and return to the source.

radiation
Light, heat, and other kinds of energy that travels in waves.

radula
The filelike tongue of some animals, such as snails.

seismograph
A machine that measures the size of earthquakes.

skeleton
The framework of a body that provides support and protection. Some animals have external skeletons, such as shells, and others, like humans, have internal skeletons made of bone.

sonar
A system of detecting objects underwater by sound pulses reflected off their surfaces.

species
A group of living organisms with similar characteristics. Individuals from the same species are capable of breeding, or producing young.

spectrum
The colors of light that we can see. The spectrum consists of the colors of the rainbow— red, orange, yellow, green, blue, indigo, and violet.

spore
One of the tiny cells that are released from fungi, which will germinate and grow into a new fungus.

starch
A carbohydrate that is often used to store energy in living organisms.

ultrasound
Very high-frequency sound.

vertebra
One of the bones in an animal's backbone.

vertebrate
An animal that has a backbone and an internal skeleton. Vertebrates include fish, amphibians, reptiles, birds, and mammals.

Index

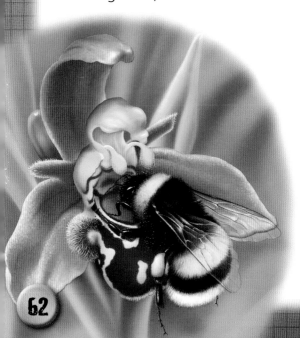

Acknowledgments

The Publisher would like to thank the following for permission to reproduce their material. Every care has been taken to trace copyright holders. However, if there have been unintentional omissions or failure to trace copyright holders, we apologize and will, if informed, endeavor to make corrections in any future edition.

Key: b = bottom, c = center, l = left, t = top

Pages 8–9 Alamy/Ryan McGinnis; 9tr Shutterstock/Ramona Heim; 11c Shutterstock/Pavle Marjanovic; 12 Shutterstock/Henryk Sadura; 13tl Shutterstock/fenghui; 13r Shutterstock.IKO; 15tr Science Photo Library (SPL)/Eye of Science; 15cb Alamy/David Bleeker; 15br Alamy/David Bleeker; 17 Shutterstock/ Clive Watkins; 19 Shutterstock/Adrian Hughes; 20br Corbis/Association Chantal Mauduit Namaste; 21tr Shutterstock/Denis & Yulia Pogostin; 23b Corbis/Lars Langemeier; 24br Shutterstock/Kaarsten; 25tl Shutterstock/Evskaya Igorevna; 26 Corbis/Jim Cummins; 27tr Shutterstock/Beerkoff; 27bl Shutterstock/Brykaylo Yuriy; 27bc Shutterstock/Tobik; 28 Shutterstock/Geanina Bechna; 28br inset SPL/Science Source; 29br Alamy/Nature Picture Library; 30cl Shutterstock/Marcel Jancovic; 30bl Shutterstock/Brian A. Jackson; 30–31 Shutterstock/Carole Castelli; 31tr Shutterstock/Darren Baker; 32–33 Shutterstock/Jeff Schultes; 33br Shutterstock/Sean Gladwell; 36r Photolibrary/Royal Armouries; 37cl Shutterstock/Terrance Emerson; 38–39 Corbis/Leif Skoogfors; 40–41 Alamy/Michael Klinec; 43tr Corbis/Norbert Wu; 43bl SPL/NASA/Science Source; 45br SPL/Ted Kinsman; 46–47 Photolibrary; 47tc Photolibrary; 48–49 NASA; 48cr Shutterstock/Eduard Harkonen; 50t Shutterstock/36clicks; 51tr Shutterstock/Jeff Hinds; 53tr SPL/Juergen Berger; 53cr Shutterstock/Joris van den Heuvel; 55br Shutterstock/Daniel Krylov; 56 Corbis/Jim Zuckerman; 57tr Shutterstock/Nuvola; 57b Shutterstock/Sergey Lavrentev

The Publisher would like to thank the following illustrators:
Robin Carter, Robin Boutell, Dan Cole, Stuart Jackson Carter, Mick Posen (all of www.The.Art.Agency.co.uk); Mark Bergin; Planman Technologies India Pvt. Ltd.